P9-CCZ-250

On This Day in Poetry History

Also by Amy Newman

Dear Editor
fall
Camera Lyrica
Order, or Disorder

On This Day in Poetry History

Poems by
Amy Newman

A Karen & Michael Braziller Book
Persea Books / New York

For Joe

DECATUR PUBLIC LIBRARY

JUL 01 2016

DECATUR, ILLINOIS

WITHDRAWN
Decatur Public Library

Copyright © 2016 by Amy Newman

All rights reserved. No part of this may be reproduced or transmitted in any form or by any means, electronic or mechanical, including photocopy, recording, or any information storage and retrieval system, without prior permission in writing from the publisher. Request for permission to reprint or make copies, and for any other information, should be addressed to the publisher:

Persea Books, Inc.
277 Broadway
New York, NY 10007

Library of Congress Cataloging-in-Publication Data
Names: Newman, Amy (Amy Lynn) author.
Title: On this date in poetry history : poems / by Amy Newman.
Description: First edition. | New York : Persea Books, 2016. | "A Karen & Michael Braziller book."
Identifiers: LCCN 2015033504 | ISBN 9780892554706 (original trade pbk. : alk = paper)
Classification: LCC PS3564.E9148 A6 2016 | DDC 811/.54–dc23
LC record available at http://lccn.loc.gov/2015033504

First edition
Printed in the United States of America
Designed by Rita Lascaro

Contents

There must be a kind of glory to it all that people coming later will wonder at. I can see us all being written up in some huge book of the age. But under what title?

— ROBERT LOWELL, TO THEODORE ROETHKE

Oh foresight foresight.

— SYLVIA PLATH

When Eight-Month-Old Elizabeth Bishop's Father Dies, Her Mother Gertrude Stops Ice Skating

When eight-month-old Elizabeth Bishop's father dies,
her mother Gertrude stops ice skating
disinclined to the blade's splintery wake,
the skate's furrow etching a tether.
She'll have to go to hospital.
She'll come and go like attention,
like the thread in a basting stitch,
and the image of her standing in the door becomes
the space in the door where she was.
It's artful to guess the color of the sky
with eyes closed, or the patterns you make
walking over wet grass. A minute later,
the grass decides itself upward. Whether you look or not,

the cows wander through town,
the dressmaker measures the eyelet,
planets deviate, snap back.
Something's wrong, like a beast in the background,
something tastes off in the milk.
Above ice-slow fish in their spiny skeletons,
water-birds proceed to the next idea,
paying no attention to the cold trees,
paying no attention to the steeple.
The spaces between them are also unfixed.

After Four-Year-Old Ted Roethke Recovers from Mastoiditis, He Wanders into the Saginaw Oat Field and Gets Lost

After four-year-old Ted Roethke recovers from mastoiditis,
he wanders into the Saginaw oat field and gets lost
among the infinite perennials. He's dressed in seersucker,
little buttons down the front, belted, small as a puppy,
a good boy. The illness had pounded a terrible drum,
and hurt him to near nothingness, cultivating
the impressionable, spongy, childhood bone.
Then the surgeon sent a scalpel ting-tinging,
showing some teeth at that agitating bloom,
that animate mass of fermentation:
out, you excited nature of infection!

Now, in the limitless field, grain flowers
hang pale, burgeoning bells on a sway of oat. At home
parents are working their ideas to the desperate bone,
scrubbing the floors with temperance.
Lost in a field somewhere near the top of North America,
Ted Roethke hears a cowbird scratch its speckled egg
into the nest of a house sparrow.
He hears a bird passively anting,
hears the rodent's rush, the owl's head
in a delicate, terrible arc,
blurring birds with ecstatic eyes,
mice scattering,
a wingless, female aphid burrowing
into the fallible, bright green,
the whole, parasitic gist of it.

Before Three-Year-Old Elizabeth Bishop Picks up a Cotton Stocking the Morning after the Great Salem Fire of 1914

Before three-year old Elizabeth Bishop picks up a cotton stocking
the morning after the Great Salem Fire of 1914,
the town had burned all night. In her room the fire cast
alternative suggestions for shapes and shading;
intricate rose seashells ribboned the walls.
The house stood like its own bell ringing,
the sky lofting cinders and ash.
The next day, char on the houses excessive as a bird's feather.
In the front yard, a woman's cotton stocking,
and everything focused down to it:
pretty, intimate, out of place.
Her mother will say *Put that down.*

A postcard from the fire shows tiny figures
murmuring, and all the trees
more subtle, veinlets, wasp-thin, dyed black.
Oh the pretty bridge is about to fall,
sinking into disrepair, my fair ladies.
The raw-boned background thinning in smolder.
History is heartrobbing undistilled,
not delicate, not indirect as the bird's eye
choosing what it needs. Look.
You can trace the village roads on onionskin,
sketch in wet barks and shade perennials.

After Two Years of Mourning, Elizabeth Bishop's Mother Screams as She Is Fitted for Her First Colorful Dress

After two years of mourning, Elizabeth Bishop's mother
screams as she is fitted for her first colorful dress.
The sound makes a frame in the quiet room,
like watercolor at the island's hem,
still blue at the edges, and not very loud.
The dress was purple like in the bible stories,
where orphans despaired among aromatic grains.
She was gone then,
steeple-reticent, demure as sky,
an imaginary rose shedding in air.
But where is the body under the dress,
holding the voice? Where is the mother's
basket of breath? The island is all sketched in,
filled with daisies. The mother returned to the hospital,
her arms full of useless flowers, the front porch
vocal with flowers. Each petal eye waxes and wanes,
each petal drops a glaze, stammering.
Wasps undertake the honeysuckle,
dipping their weighted bodies.
Their legs are pinned out for travel, suspended on stillness,
half-sinking in the numb, achromatic air.

While a Young Randall Jarrell Poses as Ganymede for a Replica of the Parthenon in Nashville, Seven-Year-Old Delmore Schwartz's Mother Rose Notices Her Husband's Car at a Roadhouse Cafe and Makes Them Pull Over

While a young Randall Jarrell poses as Ganymede
for a replica of the Parthenon in Nashville,
seven-year-old Delmore Schwartz's mother, Rose,
notices her husband's car at a roadhouse cafe
and makes them pull over so she can go in
and there he is, leaning in,
with yet another woman. Such tsuris,
but it's no surprise: life is a desire to flee
that constant pressure behind you
from the moment you leave the womb,
trying to escape from what brung you. It's labor to be alive.

Rose twists Delmore among the tables,
weaving their bodies through the space like a migratory bird
dragging what's left of her elaborate, troubled nest.
Rose, the self-tormentor, field of desire, secret planter,
carrier of the uterus to suffer torsion unto the special one,
irritator to the gods. Her impressive wave of luminescent cursing
should be carved in high relief in massive, compact limestone
so it endures, imperishable, polished and beautiful,
cold to the touch at first, and seemingly archaic,
seemingly from ruins, as is love.

In Tennessee, twelve-year-old Jarrell will pose for two sculptors
for an Olympic frieze to adorn the replica of the Parthenon
in Nashville's Centennial Park. He'll play the part of Ganymede,
the angel child, cup-bearer to the gods, who grant him immortality
because he was simply lovely. It's no different in myth:
it's how you look and who you know.

Zeus descends as a delighted, overbearing eagle
to torque Ganymede up and set him in the revolving sky,
a beautiful boy relieved of family,
released, at the whim of centrifugal gods
from the mortal residue below.

When Aurelia Schober and Otto Plath Drive Across the Country to Carson City, Nevada to Marry

When Aurelia Schober and Otto Plath drive
across the country to Carson City, Nevada to marry,
they'll stop in Reno for Otto's divorce from his first wife,
a woman he hasn't seen in 15 years.
He's also estranged from his family,
having left the Lutheran ministry
for Darwin and the natural sciences.
Darwin had imagined a moth that no one knew to exist—
with a dipping straw so long it would seem unreal—
as a lover to a pale, impossible orchid,
because the flower's long, nectarous tube
would need such a shape
to enter the white trim inflorence and navigate
that spectacular, almost implausible, curving depth
and in the process mingle pollen grains,
to generate, produce, propel, propagate, spread, extend, evolve.
The *Xanthopan morgani* will unroll its proboscis
the intense length of the Star of Bethlehem's virginal spur,
which is draped the color of wedding cream and capped
by a pouting, magnificent vaginal lip.
Such longing sends a moth
fluttering insane to Madagascar in thrall to DNA,
as if air were centrifugal and the whole thing sorcery,
and he drinks, and they coil each to each,
which is biological destiny, bent always on travail.

It is so with desire,
Otto explained to Aurelia as they courted
among a canvas of grasses powered to reproduce grasses,
under trees hiding their seeds in fruit for a chance.
As a child when he learned where bees store honey,

he tugged all he wanted, with a handmade straw,
of that candied, plural exhaust.
He'd aspired across an ocean
as a young man, captivated in the upper Midwest,
then agitated to Seattle, then Boston, and now,
hungry into her at evening, emptying out,
propelling all his prerecorded patterns in a jiggity-jig
in some release that they'll call love,
as they bracket their resources
with whatever part of this is will and intent, which ride shotgun
on the instinct and the absolute power of natural history.
Dreamy genetic material hangs somewhere, intangible elastics,
while, feverish and hovering, large and courtly,
delicate, and fixed above her,
Otto is at last refined to his instrument,
captivated, riding the design.

When Vassar Senior Elizabeth Bishop Asks Marianne Moore to the Ringling Brothers Circus

When Vassar senior Elizabeth Bishop asks Marianne Moore
to the Ringling Brothers Circus, Moore says yes.
The elephants are costumed, in pink and reds,
wear comic feathers on their headressed heads.
They sway a shuffle pattern on their pillared legs.
Hip to shoulder, a long grey line rough
with rough skin, they conjure,
blue-dark, and slow as stares.
Beneath the spangled girl on the trapeze
(out of the way, exchanging this for that),
elephants are uneasy in the adjustable real,
their pavilion sectioned to an angular sky.
In early dawn they'd been the ones
to haul the ropes, strung to old canvas,
tight to the poles, righting up this transience,
the jury-rigged home, someone's idea of joy.

The Day after the Dean of Michigan State College Admits Him to Sparrow Hospital for Rest, a Naked Theodore Roethke Barricades Himself Behind a Hospital Mattress

The day after the Dean of Michigan State College admits him
to Sparrow Hospital for rest, a naked Theodore Roethke
barricades himself behind a hospital mattress
refusing sedatives. He won't even take one
when they try to hide it in a beer.
He's working on instinct's last nerves,
a meaty bone's wisdom rides his mind.
But a brave man gives nothing away, shows a pale modern eye
to the doctors and the therapies that monkey around
in that hydroelectric century.

After his night in the woods, mute under a tree,
he'd emerged like a fawn with a stiff, drunk heart,
like Nijinsky becoming God, his body
monochrome in the silence. He slipped in.
I want to say so much and cannot find the words
Nijinsky wrote in his asylum diary,
I was sorry to leave the tree because the tree understood me.
Roethke heard it all: the abatement of bark, the stripping of it
by the tiniest bug, the needle. Underneath you, there it is.
(There's what?) That dark that sniffs your salts,
your ditch-hidden angers soaked in ethyl alcohol,
mounted on paper. (What dark?) This dark, doctor. Tune up,
listen, inhale, for Christ's sake. Don't try to pull that stuff on me,
says Roethke, sharpening his tools in the barricade,
still tender in the habit of the child, his cargo
that one luminous brain back in the brain's cave.

When Theodore Roethke Suddenly Knows What It Feels like to Be a Lion, He Enters a Diner and Orders a Raw Steak

When Theodore Roethke suddenly knows what it feels like to be a lion,
he enters a diner and orders a raw steak. It was such a good day,
nature so explicit with him, little mongrel, little flirt,
that he couldn't sleep, what with the rough, unfinished world,
so saturated with survival, it can't help itself.
It's a hothouse of kill and feed and multiply, fruit
and feather, gristle and chew and want, hunger and hunt,
drag back to the cold nest again. It has to thorn and rub
and run and burr and fly, and shake into the wind,
disperse, to seed and to root, and here it was,
patient with him while he fled into it.
Nature slipped its cool, soft hand into his,
looking at him with that knowing glance it has,
just wanting to be with him, his shirt undone,
his mouth half–open. *Where have you been all my life?*
He heard the roses, under their pinnate leaves, ripening their hips.
Nature let him in, transparent, weightless, confused,
trembling, a little wrong, but he couldn't help himself,
drunk, savage, remote, microbial, a seed in the flesh,
a tooth, sharpening, coarse, terribly honest, too good, too good,
get me down, he said, get me down off this, he told the dean,
weeping a little in his growling bones.

When Delmore Schwartz Reads about Tadpoles in Encyclopædia Britannica *at Yaddo*

When Delmore Schwartz reads about tadpoles
in *Encyclopædia Britannica*, at Yaddo,
something happens inside the stem of poetry,
something elastic, and it bends a little.
He's living through the winter in Saratoga Springs,
outside his habitat of choice,
wriggling in the histories of complicated angers,
imagining a creature unaffected by light.
Such are the options of nature, which collects
and pays out on its own time.
Thoughts accumulate and shed behind his unavailable eyes.
Somewhere in the confusing trees, a Palm Warbler
rests in its migratory path, wags a delicate tail,
and whistles so sweetly, you'd never think
of all it needs just to survive.
Even when it's calm, the resting heart's moving,
brandishing bloods, renewing itself,
depleting, renewing. Are you there,
American poetry? Isn't it exhausting?
From where he sits in the farmhouse,
Delmore's parents are indistinct as material
floating in the fluid that supports the brain,
little dots swimming in the intrathecal space,
shifting in time, and he wants his memories of them
to be remote, and pure as a child's brainstem,
tentative, involuntary, practically larval.

When John Berryman Faints in Front of the Picasso in the Museum of Modern Art

When John Berryman faints in front of the Picasso
in the Museum of Modern Art,
it's because he's so tired, he's strung out, or,
according to Delmore Schwartz, jealous,
Berryman feigning, pulling focus for spite,
having not been invited, as had Delmore,
to Auden's. Which version is true?
Delmore had a tendency to exaggerate.

Or maybe it's better to say
he dreamed about things in midair,
and why not swerve from truth's constant voice,
from the grievance so steadfast it's practically stone,
your gravel path of childhood, so absolute it's ontology.
His mother Rose insisting they pull over the car
to run into the diner where father is philandering again,
with a pretty piece of ass. Oh the shouting!
She holds Delmore's captive hand
the whole time, little prison. *Love*,
he begins, in his mind, *love, love*... He embroiders,
he makes a bible story. He was seven. So

he's used to melodrama. So when Berryman faints,
the New York story deepens, something happening
to the poetry of the early twentieth century.
They move through the present tense in bits and increments,
in imperceptible sighs, and differences,
in pigments, and by degrees,
Delmore standing, Berryman turning
to the cool museum floor. On the wall the painting
proceeds into the future tense.

It was from Picasso's Blue Period.
Everyone had had enough of that kind of sadness for a while,
but it wasn't going to disappear.

When Robert Lowell Broke Jean Stafford's Nose for the Second Time

When Robert Lowell broke Jean Stafford's nose
for the second time, something happened to poetry,
vascular, circulatory, an unstable shift in the tender stem
of the coming years,
as the introduction of sulfuric acid to soil
alters hydrangeas to a boy-child blue.
Are you alright, poetry? He hit her hard.

Her pain was exquisite and private,
a castle with seven rooms.
In the final room, the brain shivered, gem-like,
palpable as mathematics.
Doors opened, doors wavered in passive arcs,
beneath a moon unsuitable for metaphor.
What would have been the point, anyway,
of such dreaming? Against the backdrop of the unreachable
planets, pigeons navigate their evening,
soundless at such a distance, seeming graceful, yes,
but terrified, shedding almost everything naïve.

While John Berryman Rides the Cyclone at Palisades Amusement Park in New Jersey, Elizabeth Bishop Grinds Binocular Lenses at a Navy Optical Shop in Key West

While John Berryman rides the Cyclone at Palisades Amusement Park in
    New Jersey,
Elizabeth Bishop grinds binocular lenses at a Navy optical shop in Key West,
polishing surfaces smooth. Everything grinds down to smaller asperities,
each one a universe of seeing. There's a joy to labor,
placing the mind where the machine says, fusing and attending the eye,
the binoculars merging left and right, agreeing on what exists
while you look there. Astronomers used telescopes because
looking through a God-made eye can only get you so far.
The man-made lens magnifies the real we couldn't see,
though to magnify, angled one way, can also be to burn.

When John Hershel made his telescopes, refining each curved lens,
he came to understand that a liquid's smooth surface
bears a relation to a surface artificially polished
as does a mirror to a ploughed field:
human labor trying for something sublime.
Oh that's beautiful! Bishop thinks,
watching one grain of dust lift from the polishing lens
and seemingly disappear, to climb in a way too small for us to see,
for our inability to pin down what we then call nothingness.
Why else create a heaven in a precise shade of blue,
this optical advantage made by waves of our own reflected light?

In New Jersey, John Berryman rides the Cyclone at Palisades Amusement
    Park
with his wife Eileen, escaping for the day the ugly summer,
scouring for jobs, finally selling encyclopedias door-to-door,
which feels a little bit like scraping ruts in an uneven earth,
as if the flesh that holds his fluids and bones,

jangling his body through the sales territory like keys,
can sell you a series of books, one word
rubbing up against the next, one idea pissing off the next.
A set of encyclopedias should really be called
a collection of everything it's possible to know,
and the heart just sinks right there. *Goddammit Eileen.*
As they rise above the cliffs named because they resemble something that,
close-up, they were not, the Berrymans drift toward the attractive sky
—a blue unknowable, a blue trick, one capricious blue on a spectrum
of possible blues. The coaster's cars abrade the track,
seem to break and buckle, for Christ's sake, this fear
astringent and holy, and he soaks in the terrible wonderful,
his pom-de-pom heart polishing to nothing,
almost vanishing, abraded to a *yes* at the tippy-top.
Guilty he pleads, as the world falls away.

After Robert Lowell Starves Himself for Lent, a Seaplane Deposits Gertrude Buckman on Loon Islet and She Swims Across the Lake

After Robert Lowell starves himself for Lent,
a seaplane deposits Gertrude Buckman on Loon Islet
and she swims across the lake to the Lowells' house,
quicksilver, cagey, newly cleansed. In that moment,
there were many overlapping arcs of narrative:
The Piper Cub tipping a blithe, sunlit wing as it approached,
the swimming woman's jeweled strokes
gaining on the acreage in capillary waves,
the occasional birdsong veining the air.
Everything soaked in its own design.
Did you get all that, American poetry?
It was as if this world were shaped by a God
dissatisfied, parental, bullheaded and crafty,
with time on His Hands, and what should He do but
gather in the materials, tuck this here, double it onto itself
in pleats and pliable energies, crease and fold
this origami of sin and green transcendence?
The thought of it leaves you all strung up, a guilt
digging at your heart like butcher twine,
leaving a mark around the whole bloody, sopping package.
For Lent, Lowell had starved himself into a harsh,
demanding purity, a see-through purity, the kind of pure
that sees the face of God move across the waters.
As he watches Gertrude infringe onto the dock,
the lake sheds her body in ecstatic rivulets,
while above them in a thrilling, postlapsarian tree,
one gray catbird hides, about to sing again.

Elizabeth Bishop Sails Across the Equator at Night

At just the right time of the year here,
if the sun were directly above,
you'd cast no shadow. How marvelous
to be relieved of the body's crowding secrets.
On Easter as a child she saw perplexing sugar eggs,

cut for side view to a panorama,
an icing scene: a curving sky, beneath which sat
a happy rabbit perched in whimsy,
frosted in silence there. And she felt recognized,
a latent center concealed with sugars.

Crossing the equator at night,
the vague freighter plows waves
repetitive and tight as the scales of a fir cone,
that cabinet of seed that responds to change.
What heat might surprise her open, finally?
Oh the hours and passages of such demeanor!

In a Russian tale, the Emperor's gift to his love
is an egg crosshatched in enamel waves.
The shell opens first to a golden yolk, and within the yolk,
a jeweled hen. And on the hen's tiny head,
a diamond miniature of the royal crown.

How this tiny majesty diverts; one turns way
from the sad histories. Now the ship
passes over that imaginary circle that divides the earth
in two, like the seam of a Fabergé egg,
and she turns, navigating the hinge.

When Delmore Schwartz Drives His Buick Roadmaster Through the Holland Tunnel, He Imagines Walt Whitman Behind the Wheel

When Delmore Schwartz drives his Buick Roadmaster through the
    Holland Tunnel,
he imagines Walt Whitman behind the wheel, meaty,
gorgeous on the upholstered double-depth Foamtex cushioning,
advancing his everythings within the bright concavity
of 6,000 horsepower motors forcing air through
that's right the United States of the ventilation fans,
93 feet underwater in the first mechanical underwater tube
in the world. America's childhood eye is the naïve eye
that loves you, loves the greeny pastoral
and the deer leaping, and the prairie grass,
cantering out of the forties, that dew-sparkling,
mother-loved-you childhood, just as it was for you,
so it was for me—the empties scattering on the swerves,
the Seconal calming like the solid yellow lines—
And now we proceed generations toward our future
in the vehicle of progress oh thou master of the road,
essentially the greatest poem, its centrifugal spokes spinning,
and the hand of the machine is the hand of my own body
and the spirit of the automobile's gleaming chrome crossbows
against the scallops of landscape on both sides
is the shield of the army of my own heart like a tick-tock gargoyle,
and the bright fireball combustion of 170 horsepower
is my muscle coursing by the foundry chimneys,
the past sliding on ball bearings and blood,
on invisible sprockets kapoketa poketa
poketa newsreels b&w history where the mother waits
patiently for the best son in the world to come home and then
there he is home in his uniform, and everyone cries,
we all cry at the end, that's why we call it the end,
even though it's a beginning, in another way,

Delmore thinks, inside his holy egg carton of a head,
as he emerges on the Jersey side, those wild, pulse-crazy arms
powering the steering mechanism left and right, like he's going places.

When Delmore Schwartz Looks out the Window of R. P. Blackmur's Princeton Office, Which Delmore's Using while Blackmur Is away

When Delmore Schwartz looks out the window of R. P. Blackmur's
    Princeton office,
which Delmore's using while Blackmur is away,
a common pigeon lands on the sill. Separated by glass,
on the outside, the pretty one, anxious and lost.
The heart's ballistics panic the future.
What's captivity? The mother cage in the brain,
or that stingy heart, engine of the whole aerobic flight?
What's paradise to the exile but the past,
which was not paradise? The mother country
blurred her complaints all over you, and there you are,
in someone else's territory, with someone else's books,
tapping cigarette ash into a Savarin can, the smoke
wandering toward the window where a pigeon
perches on tense, crimson feet.
When Mary and Joseph fled into Egypt,
they stopped to rest in an inhospitable,
cheerless, cynical desert dark, a barren,
fruitless dark. In such a dark (the cut-dead dark,
the forsaken dark, the exile's unproductive dark)
you need what they had, the baby god, warm as knish,
bird-small, content, certain, unashamed of you,
its candle power fluttering your bones, its tiny head
iridescent with love and asking nothing.

When Robert Lowell Tosses His Eyeglasses
out of the Window of the Payne Whitney Clinic

When Robert Lowell tosses his eyeglasses
out of the window of the Payne Whitney clinic,
Thorazine frames the tumble to slow motion.
The glitter of the glass reducing, transforming,
like money distilling to distress,
like body vaporized to spirit,
the alchemy shaping what it carries. Delight!
Payne Whitney was a *Gothic bride, all arches,*
groins and stone lace-work, narrow,
shaping chaos like a sonnet
but in syringes, in straightjackets.
The frames rework a metaphor in air,
bright absolutes of freedom seriatim
end over end, lucky, failing,
little avalanche, dear agitating heart, free
like a kingfisher flashing open the bright red
inside blood to catch some air,
and guilty, free and guilty.

When the Boy Arrives with a Telegram for John Berryman, Berryman Turns to His Student Phil Levine and Asks, "Are You John Berryman?"

When the boy arrives with a telegram for John Berryman,
Berryman turns to his student Phil Levine and asks,
"Are you John Berryman?"
No, says Levine. *Then I must be*, says Berryman,
taking the telegram's white folded sheets,
the long-distance transmission from elsewhere.
Distance was Berryman's thing.
His father, John Smith Sr., had shot himself,
the bullet conveying the gun's explosive distance to his chest.

In Tampa Bay, when he'd tried to drown,
he took Berryman's brother Bob out to sea with him,
the two absorbed into the low, far horizon.
Now that's a good example of distance
right there; that's a humdinger.
On the beach, women screamed
but they vibrated into nothings,
into absence, because Bob and his father,
just so gone, were too far out, unreceptive,
and their eyes were not reading the shore for love.
Later, Smith kills himself outside the apartment,
and mother remarries 10 weeks later,
and Berryman gets his new name.

How far we have come from the optical telegraphs,
smoke signals, beacons, and semaphore lines,
where you'd send something into the air
and hope that it was received,
because someone was already looking for you,
their eyes scanning the whole leased acreage of the sky,
because nobody entirely disappears. *Are you John Berryman?*

His father had taken his brother for a swim.
So it had been Bob and not he whom his father had chosen.
What can be deciphered from the centuries of air and salt,
from maps and old news, from your terror,
from an encyclopedia or the folded page
that someone declares is history?

When John Berryman Threw an Empty
Bottle of Scotch at Philip Levine's Head

When John Berryman threw an empty bottle of scotch
at Philip Levine's head, he used a kind of pitching motion,
tossing the heavy glass end over end.
He swings it. He whips it.
It was because Franny, Levine's girl, had a skirt on,
and under that skirt, Berryman knew,
were miracles and sweet healing waters.
Under every skirt lurks a potential sonnet,
a faraway, an estate, the wiry gardens patterning wildly,
the iambs of thigh against thigh grasping,
but not in possession, no: rejoicing!
Let's say, instead: rejoicing! He could get in there
and wear her like a long white glove. Should he?
He should! He should not!
Dear feudal castle your lord and master seeks a feel,
let me in, said his hand,
I seek, his hand said, *protection from my enemies.*
He's fortified. When Berryman tosses the bottle,
it moves like a pinwheel, and nobody knows this but him,
because it's a sucker punch. It's a beaut, though:
the glass fascinates in the kitchen light,
factoring helixes across the cupboards in topspin,
nosediving into Levine, laying him out.
Berryman stomps his hand. But they're men in 1953.
American poetry eyes the base, threads a needle,
breathes, shakes a tail feather.

While Sylvia Plath Hemorrhages after Losing Her Virginity in Cambridge, Robert Lowell Jumps from a Moving Taxicab in Cincinnati

While Sylvia Plath hemorrhages after losing her virginity,
Robert Lowell jumps from a moving taxi cab in Cincinnati,
because he doesn't have money to pay the fare.
He'd been at the Gaiety Theater to watch Rose La Rose
play hide-and-seek with her unseen lands
eclipsing that new world so it glints through her costume,
a wild horse between unbearably shiny trees.
The need, the desire to enter those hips is resolute,
like the Mayflower pilgrims drawn across the Atlantic
to ravish a paradise, to plant themselves within.
When Rose La Rose's iambic ass bangs its affirmation of life,
it narrates the history of the Puritans in North America
from The Great Migration to the Roger Williams controversy.

In Cambridge, Plath is bleeding after rough sex,
a scary red, the red of too much, a deep romantic blur,
a velvety red of a fake rose, which, like her,
is artful: produced and modified by skill and labor.
It takes work to be female in the fifties.
To rid yourself of your hangnail virginity
is one step closer to undoing the figurative,
like a Pollack painting's distillation to energy
and then, the eventual loss of shine.
It's ironic nostalgia to be alive, tumbling forward
from an Edenic past, while the ones without childhoods
were Adam and Eve. Did you see that coming, American poetry?
A woman smuggled a flower out of a garden
between her powerful legs, and nothing's changed.
Things are always on the verge
of spilling, as if escaping the present moment
could bring, one fine day, whatever you see in front of you,
call it forgiveness, call it freedom or delight.

Sylvia Plath Is on the Night Train from Paris

with a lover asleep and the Olivetti
on the floor of the compartment.
The dark unfolding outside the window
is an infinite religious space.
Her mind branches, trying out crashing,
inadequate metaphors.

Just days ago, she had changed one word
in a problem line, leaving noun for adjective,
describing the end, not the means.
Then such a silvery-white there was!
The language transformed, ductile, like metal.
That was arrival, novitiate, your darling cell.

The train leans into lightening sky.
To her left are lemon trees, yolk-yellow
relenting fruit, and pastel houses
on exquisite, fertile land. Close-up,
the bright flowers purge their seeds,
tiny, crisp coats flung finally out.

On the right, the Mediterranean
forces itself repeatedly in blue,
carrying on under an adamant sun.
There had been a moon in the night, hadn't there,
a romantic spot on the eye somewhere?
But who remembers such dopiness,

given this vertebral infinite, this agitation?
On the other side of this sea is Egypt,
where the girl saint evaporated to a pureness,
while the anchorite suffered his body,
combustible in devotion, and giving up.
Now the train unloads every inch of the past,

absolving in a lustrous violence.
She would like to be taken by force
into the terrible sea
for the malice that powers the heart for real,
and shaken until she sees stars, snarling white,
abrasive and well-meaning.

Sylvia Plath Is in Paris With a Balloon on a Long String

Sylvia Plath is in Paris with a balloon on a long string,
its tricolor streamers floating and trailing.
It takes up the air like a determined child.
Plath was riding her horses of need,
and then breaking them, one by one.
The horse of loneliness, the horse of panic.
The horse of the Sacre Coeur's calcite-and-rainwater white
piped on Montmartre like a wedding cake.
The horse of the wallpaper powdered with rosebuds.
The horse of weeping in the charming vestibule.
The horse of the park's green geometry,
of the mushroom's black underpleats.
The horse of the lily-of-the-valley's chaste bell.
The horse of the prickly thin storm about to be,
of the cool cottons of the hotel bed
and his beautiful body, golden, lean,
and the horse of having been so close,
and then changing his mind.
The horse of her will like a planet, irrefutable,
distantly tethered to the bestial earth, and Paris
splayed and blazing around them, as if illustrated.

While Sylvia Plath Studies The Joy of Cooking on Her Honeymoon in Benidorm, Spain, Delmore Schwartz Reclines in the Front Seat of His Buick Roadmaster

While Sylvia Plath studies *The Joy of Cooking* on her honeymoon in
    Benidorm, Spain,
Delmore Schwartz reclines in the front seat of his Buick Roadmaster
listening to a Giants game on the car radio.
The car's parked on his farmland in Baptistown,
New Jersey, where obstinate plants attempt survival
at great odds, their vital spikes insulting and defending.
The thistle fans its prickly leaves,
the burdock hustles, miserly. Its dry-as death-seed
will outlast you, traveler, its dry-as-hope seedling will use you,
tenacious as the leftover god, the eye-of-the-needle-god,
the straggly one, the Shylock, who lent you your life,
who chose this desert wilderness for exile.
He manifests the empty field for you to wander.
He removeth your brilliance and set you in a basket
alone among the rushes. He maketh the coral of Seconal
and suffers you to recline in the evergreen Dexamyl shade,
while Ernie Harwell calls the last out
(Willie Jones popping up to Al Dark)
in the car's radium glow. Do you see it, American poetry?
The happy arc of the ball above Shibe Park—
a moment of promise falling off, coming to nothing.
Disappearing to atoms. Giants win, 4-2.

In Benidorm, Plath skins the market rabbit, hind to head.
She'll flour and sear the taut pink flesh
and scrape the carrots naked. Spain is a million things,
it's lantanas and hibiscus, it's roses that aren't ashamed
to split their skirts for love, rude flowers pushing out of their skins,
and all-new vines hugging the old walls, new ascendancy,

shooting up into skies like something about to matter.
The peppercorns that season the stew grow in clusters
like glands, ripening, and within each pod is the seed,
the hard, dry, concentrated bitterness for which it is prized.

When Patricia Hartle Would Give Delmore Schwartz a Ride to His Old Farm Property in New Jersey, He Would Wander about in the Fields for Hours, Calling for a Lost Cat

When Patricia Hartle would give Delmore Schwartz a ride
to his old farm property in New Jersey,
he would wander about in the fields for hours,
calling for a lost cat named Riverrun,
after the first word of *Finnegan's Wake*.
Schwartz was a fan of Joyce, Schwartz was a scholar,
hidden in language, or content there,
his high, bright intelligence
candling ideas over his whitened mind
like a war factory once the war had ended.

The past is a field so full of errors,
he wanders agitating like a heart muscle.
Riverrun, he calls, part wet human air,
in a field so highly allergic, so raw with pollens,
the random ashes dust his forehead,
flourish him with weeds.
It is pretty to see from here,
a poet wandering in a field of yellows,
singing to the cat, who must be elsewhere.
An imagined animal must be loved,
safe and missing him, distracted in the shade.

When Anne Sexton Makes Enough Money Selling Beauty Counselor Cosmetics Door-to-Door, She Buys James Wright's The Green Wall

When Anne Sexton makes enough money selling Beauty Counselor
    Cosmetics door-to-door,
she buys James Wright's *The Green Wall*,
winner of the Yale Younger Poets Series for 1957.
It's a reward for all those afternoons
crossing the transom into a stranger's home,
moving from the fresh-cut lawn's perfect green
to the housewife's fenced-in field of a heart.
The new lipstick brightens your mouth into an Oh.
Every she who dwells in the suburban kingdom
knows the bedtime story of the prince who loved you
among the glades beneath the tree's tiresome, ripening fruit,
the disinterested doves lamenting what they know.
His love-from-a-distance-glance, his nervous-tender-glory,
I saw you and I had to know you, dark eyes,
the handsome hand tightening on your bouquet of pinks,
of whatever you've got hidden up there, and whatever it is,
it really gets in the way.
Anne's black patent leather sample case on her arm
is shell pink on the inside, a promising pink,
lighter than the pink of a mouth, much less pink than the womb,
that impure, luxurious vessel, that cave of causes,
that pink trapdoor, frilly as a corsage.
But you have to look closer, American poetry.
The sealed-for-freshness housewife heart
sends out her wild response anyway, and what comes of it
is worth your time. When the dove flies off, there's all that wingwork,
whistling. Sexton and Wright, sometime in the future,
will dance in a kitchen, giddy with love,
whitish hands covered in cookie flour, kissing to Sibelius,
also happily ever after, also once upon a time.

When Delmore Schwartz Tells William Phillips that the Voices in His Head Are Coming from the Top of the Empire State Building

When Delmore Schwartz tells William Phillips that the voices in his head
are coming from the top of the Empire State Building,
they look up toward the steeple rising 1,453 feet and 8 and 9/10 inches
above New York, the flesh on their necks creasing.
The pinnacle at building's top is a lightening rod,
poking a delicate *so what* too close to the Farbissen Eye
of Delmore's punishing, nagging, and abandoning God.
Was that it, American poetry? Maybe that was it.
Beneath the late 1950's fabric, their hearts strike repeatedly
in their chests: relaxing, contracting, the A-OK American blood
Dexamilled to a human shape, their Arrow shirts
tapering up toward their unavoidable brains.
Delmore's high, bright facade,
that crèche of a face, cycles its paraffin features
on his illuminated manuscript of a head.
She grew large in the third month and could hide him no longer.
She made a basket of bulrushes and placed him in it,
by the softening riverbank. Who drew him out of the waters?
Take this child away, he mutters, candling his eyes upward.
The nation's hanging radio towers, wiring for infinities,
O advanced wilderness!
The ad for Dexedrine Sulfate reads: *New life for the living*
beneath the photograph of men holding golf clubs of optimism,
smoking cigarettes of well-being,
their sadness pared to a Tom Thumb rage so slender,
you can dissolve it under your tongue,
and rinse it with the yes of Miltown, in your cycling veins,
and rinse it again with Phenobarbital's yes,
and you're golden, you're fatted calf, you're milk and honey.

While Anne Sexton and Her Daughters Peer Through the Window to Scan the Sky for Santa Claus, Robert Lowell Watches William Carlos Williams' Train Leave Boston Station

While Anne Sexton and her daughters peer through the window
to scan the sky for Santa Claus,
Robert Lowell watches William Carlos Williams' train leave Boston Station,
retreating in an acute angle among the snowflakes' perfect, perishing forms.
The train is resolving to the past tense, with Williams inside
like a narrowing messiah, gone to the cave only halfway through the myth.
If the train carrying Williams leaves the station, traveling 50 mph,
and Lowell's dexterous heart beats at 60 mph,
at what time will that package of blood, that aqueduct of will,
wired up with arteries like a transistor radio, contracting its syllables,
pass Williams' train? And what then?
What is that manic organ for, if not to pace enthralled in the body,
to document a provisional cortege of belief
to the exhausting, see-through sky?

Through the upstairs window of their house in Newton Lower Falls,
Anne Sexton and her daughters scan the sky for Santa Claus.
Who doesn't love that temporary splendor of belief
that might appear above the variegated world, in an easter of arrivals?
In the bedtime stories it was always touch and go,
the prince longing for you, having scoured the world
having suffered intensely, because you deserved his love,
or the children in the cottage made of cake and icing,
waiting for God, and starved to the childish bone.
All legends begin with a wound that hurts
the latent oblivion that is any door opening.
Mingled with flesh, everything is metaphor:
the steeple's arrow scratching at the hiding place,
the advent calendar's striptease,
Anne narrating, for her daughters, a tinsel eden,

a season of happiness in a finite space.
Look up in the sky, poetry! Maybe he's there,
aloof, suffering, returning, and Anne
dreams of him, flirts with the idea of him,
the stubborn one who loves her anyway, the one who got away.

When Her Mother Lay Dying, Anne Sexton Took a Portable Radio out of the Hospital Room

When her mother lay dying, Anne Sexton
took a portable radio out of the hospital room,
its plastic pleats marking her palm.
She could hear the muscles beneath her skin there
arguing yes, saying *abductor* and *flexor*,
take and *bend*, *steal* and *move*,
calculating the formula for navigation,
for the audible hot of just wanting and having,
beyond the linoleum.
                              She stepped gracefully,
ceremonially, as the doctors monitored
her lovely behind, its signal amplifying
into the space as travels. Oh attraction!
A bride conveys her wet box of secrets
all the way down the long aisle.
She is frilled like a lamb in disinterested whites,
her cap of lace muffling like applause:
thrilling, confusing, like the transistor's
enthusiastic static. What does it mean?
A bride moves down the aisle in waves,
shifting the voltage with each leg's click.

Here comes the rest of it, ladies,
the underneaths and pushes,
the skin and sweat and the sinews,
vegetation shooting roots at will,
playing the surfaces, drifting for contact,
touching and mewling. The insides
are bundled and wired for history's cold surface.
The portable radio hums like a child,
clicks sharp when she switches it on or off,
and it sings at her, it makes all sorts of cries for her.

After Lecturing on Modern American Poetry In Delhi, John Berryman Visits the Cuttack Leprosarium

After lecturing on modern American poetry in Delhi,
John Berryman visits the Cuttack Leprosarium,
chastened by a hangover so distinct
he could title it. The quarantine seems peaceful,
a time-lapse of bruises rising on skin,
the micro bacteria's spheres and rods and spirals
scavenging each leper's body with textures,
stubborn gray paisleys and slow, aggressive stars.

India is an exotic of blood and ash
undulant with birds, profound with suffering
and acceptance so lake-sleek, so glassily still,
grace might float down as a heron
to gaze into the placid human crush.
But the songs in their terrors are systemic.
They undress him inside the flesh, hem to his haw.
Sadness strips to its parasites,
shivers in worms, smokes his Tareytons.

The lepers salaam in their purgatory.
With their warning chimes, they are like monks,
tithing through red gills and smoke oh grace & they ignore
how godawful the body feels, they divest,
they translate to something without bones, or weight,
something rose-like, crisp, what's the phrase,
what in Christ's name are you getting at,
Berryman? He is unhinging.
His older-than-it-should-be heart
ba-booms a turbulence like a deep-sea fish,
rolling, wide-mouthed, out of place,
all systems rinsed in pain, in terrible oxygen.

Revising a Poem, Anne Sexton Thinks about Mercy

Favored by angels, Lot stands
yards from the rude ones, brutes
stumbling to his strange door.
This is the free space, the step-by-step
by which the tale ascends.

Everything's made human by its flaw.
The angels are ready for sleep,
having arrived as if through a channel,
their imaginary bodies buoyant in thistle,
and animals nearby, murmuring straw.

Should she pursue, with her eye
for the mercy on which the Bible's tenderness
hangs like a myth in ether? Your crookedness
forgiven, liabilities exposed.
A careless angel, transparent, nearby

admitting that notch of light
so you may offer your human throat
for the beast to note each craving error.
The light forcing that affliction open.
Imagine a body absolved, salt-white

narrative, calm and devout:
your opposite, your mirror life.
Anne had been inelegant, wife
in a honeycomb of illness,
and poetry took her hand, led her out.

Yet others writhe behind. Bible studies
overlook the passage where Lot
offers his virgin daughters to the crowd
in infinite cold terms. And in Judges,
we pass over the concubine, cut in pieces,

bloody. (How these quieted obsessions arrive.
You can scour the ruins where angels
gazed elsewhere, and angry men
fought and fucked the narrative.
Her side of that story did not survive.)

This is why, in the holy book,
Lot's wife looks back in the narrative,
why she disregards you, angel, denying
your neglect. How she whirls, revising
herself visible in the story. Look.

While Assia Wevill Studies the London Evening Standard for an Apartment to Sublet, John Berryman Disagrees with a Nun at His Summer Seminar about her Interpretation of a Passage from "Song Of Myself"

While Assia Wevill studies the *London Evening Standard*
for an apartment to sublet, John Berryman disagrees with a nun
about her interpretation of "Song Of Myself."
She's puzzled by Whitman's integration of body and soul
because it erases boundaries, and he's all ego, isn't he?
Is not the silence of God's absence immiscible? she asks.
Does the poet understand the effort it takes to erase the self for such love?
Berryman, idiosyncratic with flesh,
receives the infinite soul of a blessed Tareyton into his body
while he imagines the nun's immateriality
beneath her tabernacle of robes, her words
washed in those perfect lungs,
forced from her guileless throat to the room
like tiny Adams and Eves fleeing a picket-fence Eden.
That was a time, pal, that crossing over, the flesh got tender,
purity of heart complicated with a twitchy lust,
the world got its trouble-de-doo, got all its metaphors.
Wasn't Christ—wriggling, obscured, in darkness,
up all night, troubled, abandoned—one enormous wound?
And doesn't flesh open endlessly,
each striated tendon bathed in blood,
that same lacquery red as his eyelid's inside?
Born from this air, sister, every atom as good belongs.

In London, Assia studies the paper and chooses 3 Chalcot Square,
where Ted and Sylvia lean their red, impatient souls
into each other's cleaving body. Plath's desire is exquisite,
a root bathed in the waters of bitterness,
righteous as inflammation, trailing sin like hair.

In Massenet's *Thais*, the shivering girl gives up her lust
to walk, andante religioso, into a dessert,
the parched bliss of dispossession which is eternal life,
but the monk wants her, Ooh la la!
That's the trouble! The heart's articulate slaughterhouse
is so rosy with wanting, it goes all the way to the bony bone.
Assia's legs, hinged open at the mainspring,
begin their slow release of power forward.
I celebrate myself, the doorbell says.

By the Time John Berryman Bails Delmore Schwartz out of Jail after the National Poetry Festival In Washington DC, the Trees at Court Green Have Uttered Their Leaves all over England

By the time John Berryman bails Delmore Schwartz out of jail
after the National Poetry Festival in Washington, DC,
the trees at Court Green have uttered their leaves
all over England. Hughes' mistress calls,
and Plath rips out the phone with one brisk tug.
She had decorated for her mother's arrival,
painting intricate, perfect flowers on the hive,
while the bees agitate in perplexed sweetness.
It had been a spring so terrifyingly lovely,
the laburnum's armies of gold, the cherry's vicious red
suffused, like a heart muscle sliced open for splendor.
And why not study the beating thing, its chock-full,
bouquet-of-roses fiction, emptying and refilling,
its up-to-here nectars cycling?

After Berryman posts bail in Washington,
a bewildered Delmore escapes him,
propels his pinion gear madness into a cab,
bright, mackereled fury on his kiosk of a head
like bunting, waving, disheveling.
What's the best way to get there, he asks the cabdriver,
the head or the heart? From the cab's window,
the change of seasons is almost pretty.
The cherry trees, having lost their virgin pinks,
are the fiery, pissed-off color of something all wised-up.

When Robert Lowell Fell in Love With the Stewardess on the Flight to Asunción

When Robert Lowell fell in love with the stewardess
on the flight to Asunción,
having ruined things in Brazil
by insulting a general
and arm-wrestling Rafael Alberti,
and reading the entire *Life Studies* to an audience,
all the way through
with no comments in between,
he had already thrown away his medication,
revising himself out of that outline,
had taken off his clothing to climb naked
on the statues of the horses in Buenos Aires.

Above the city named for the acceptance of the physical body
of the Virgin Mary into heaven,
and held in the plane's apparatus of logic,
its frame of sheet metal like a stanza
delighted in roll, pitch, and yaw,
he wanted buoyancy, sea-change,
he wanted to be a vessel of agitation launching skyward,
something heavier than air wrenching
against air. The silver dynamics of flight
pierced him like fact. His breath
worked its clock magic and the girl's legs
shaped air with their strokes, like a hummingbird's.

While John Berryman Drives In His Orange Chevrolet Through a Minnesota Rainstorm to Lecture on Don Quixote, Sylvia Plath Paints the Beehives of Court Green

While John Berryman drives in his orange Chevrolet through a Minnesota
    rainstorm
to lecture on *Don Quixote*, Sylvia Plath paints the beehives of Court Green,
stroking one stern white coat after another on the hive,
the cave house of sweet, angry, unimpressed bees.
She loves the moony girls who spring out and fly back, fluttering,
exhausted, coated in powder like prom queens, frantic with labor.
You tolerate drones only so far, a stingless, stumbling breed,
flying their flag in a risk for glory two hundred feet in the air.
Who hasn't faked interest to see how far a man would go,
how charged it is under the skirt, articulate with hum?
The queen is somewhere like that just once, doomed by a slippery
resilient lust, her red-gold chase, her compound eye.
Why would you need to see everything, the landscape
retreating beneath you, all because of desire?

In Minnesota, Berryman sees clouds close enough to curse.
He's tired as he powers forward, thinking how,
when a woman walks, her rump's a honey ham, a crescent
beneath that scratchy fabric of her hose and how you watch it work,
and when you do, pal, the whole background fades to sedation.
He's tilting again, every grass blade of his uneven heart idling
beneath the rain's watery, convex drop, inside the storm's
concussive, brilliant, bending shot glass of air.
Berryman knew convexity: the way a heaven can appear
on the inside of your eyelid; how reflection in a mirror
is half self-portrait, half world.
Whatever you look at looks right back at you, pal,
sees something a million times lovelier, maybe.
Onward, dilating heart of well-meaning!

Bestir, resolute soldier, my stiffening, soaked champion!
At home he's got two linear feet of a manuscript, sifting,
breaking like dirt under the plow into freshness.
He's been writing for years like a monk in a cell,
except for the whiskey: prayerful, electric, storing it up.

After Sylvia Plath Kicks out Ted Hughes, Elizabeth Bishop Watches Idly from a Balcony in Rio as Police Chase a Thief over Picturesque Hills

After Sylvia Plath kicks out Ted Hughes in England,
Elizabeth Bishop watches idly from a balcony in Rio
as police chase a thief over picturesque hills.
The fleeing man is effervescent in those exotic, congested glades,
but he's distinct, as a grassland sparrow's song is distinct:
if you try, you can hear the tiny voice
singing its hunger, like everything else.
You can lean into the sound over those brutal hills
where the blind roots host their parasites
and the rain serves the blind roots, and nature
ransacks everything, just to get along.
Brazil perseveres in a detailed breeze,
while the sky waits with a patience so infinite,
uninterested in the open mouths, in the cricket
or the crocodile. Bishop calls to her love through the rooms
like that bird that always sounds lost.

            In London, it's winter, and Plath
is filing down hunger to the necessary bone. His absence
is the blood gap cupped violet at the artery,
he's the death vow's strapping, gigantic ache.
The children's' call sounds for her through the walls,
a sea tipped with tiny bells. Plath's ignited heart
is radiant as a priest's. She is absurd with flu,
the virus riding her proteins obsessive and eyeless,
master plunderer, unloading its stuff in glittery bits,
champion. It's a parasite of impressive abundance,
hungry at a cellular level, binding and shedding,
inevitable and determined, like everything else.

In October Plath Wakes Early,

the dawn outside gathering its wet edges.
She'd been thinking about Yeats,
tumbled in threaded dreaming,
shuffling every idea until she woke.
Summer left everything tangled,
the bean plants high like champions.
Now the Michaelmas daisy rolls in childish mounds,

its yellow eye suffused by insects scouring,
wings battering in familiar, impulsive love.
The moths have come a long way on instinct,
exhausting the seed head to relic.
They are cruel in their involuntary need
like the Magi who traveled toward turbulence
beneath a coherence of stars.

Plath watches the moths hover and sip.
Had Mary labored under God's obligation,
His miracle theater, His sticky sleight of hand?
Was He among her like bees?
There was a flare, and later, delighted angels,
and the Christ child a fuel on Mary's heart.
How the candled infant soothed the unsatisfied ones!

Later, the Magi will cleanse the furniture of that nativity,
sweep the grass from the stall's crimson floor,
simplify Mary in that old amnesia. If it all was so,
her pain must have been so exquisite,
it could be etched in limestone
until the invention of an alphabet.
She is empty to them as a space between eras,
and beautifully pale, an eclipse.

In the Hospital, Sister Marcelina Asks Lota if She Believes in God

Mais ou menos, Lota says, turning to Elizabeth,
aiming for accuracy. Belief is precisely more or less,
a motion at an edge, the surface tension of the water
charming silver against the pressure of air.

The priest in his accuracy, more or less,
bends to the altar to love from his distance,
holds a white candle to a sore throat, blessing,
decorating with light. Nothing prepared us

for the adornment of life with disaster. As a girl,
Sister Marcelina wore a crown of white roses,
spouse of Christ in her more or less accurate love,
her capricious heart motivated,

beating and cohering. She was happiest,
dressed in her garments of the anchorite,
offering her soul in its most accurate way to Christ,
in Whose gentle Eyes she perceived His suffering of love,

for which there is no metaphor, so that will have to do.
Which of Christ's memories would He choose
for His children's bedtime stories? Something golden,
decorated with animals, more or less true.

When, at the Close of Her Letter about Her Therapist Linking Suicide to Masturbation, Anne Sexton Writes, "I Shall now Go out to a New Kitchen and Prepare Shrimp and Cocktail Sauce"

When, at the close of her letter about her therapist
linking suicide to masturbation, Anne Sexton writes,
"I shall now go out to a new kitchen
and prepare shrimp and cocktail sauce," she's not kidding.
Earnest as butane is our Anne, an armory stacked
with tightly bound sticks and softened flammable powders.
Iced lettuce heads crisp in the icebox, the shrimp bray
in cold coral stripes, bright as Clairol's Frost,
those metallic nail colors coating the decade.
In the ad, an anonymous hand has long, tapered fingers
like Anne's, the wet polish licking the edge of a perfect,
rounded sheath. *Instant Icing*, the copy reads,
and it frosts like 40 below. With her tan, she could wear
a spicy coral mouth, pearls resting moist
in her neck's bone shallows. Through cocktail hours
she moves, oyster-mysterious, promising openings,
utterly naked under opal enamels,
hiding and flashing her wilds, a fluttering,
romantic, unsteady balance
like Botticelli's Venus, such a cliché for beauty,
you don't notice the sorrow right away.
Her expression is Anne's: a kindling,
a refinery in there, fuel of dark eye
shimmering down to its carbons.

When Robert Lowell Sets up Housekeeping with
Latvian Dancer Vija Vetra on West 16th Street

When Robert Lowell sets up housekeeping
with Latvian dancer Vija Vetra on West 16th Street,
this time even he doesn't know why. At St. Clement's
he had watched as she prepared Indian sacred dances for the liturgy,
shifting a series of stable categories into shapes
that twitched the bound and pinned-up heart,
the fastened-to-the-body, sequenced heart.

Her hands in a prayer shape to the face and the waist,
then held together in a scoop, become
a full-bloomed lotus, elephant-apple,
turning around, breasts,
sorrow from separation, a mirror,
village, anger, a lake,
the saddest full moon, hair falling.

Miltown is a little like wine, softening,
suffering unto the synapses. The categories relaxed,
street anger abrading the blood in powders.
He was falling in love with strangers again,
draining of everything past, simplifying,
rough-winged, hurrying for passion,
thinned to a needle, tangible as God.

On Safari in the Serengeti with Her Husband Kayo, Anne Sexton Writes Letters to Her Therapist

On safari in the Serengeti with Kayo, Anne Sexton writes letters
to her therapist, with whom she is having an affair.
While Kayo hunts, she types in the Land Rover,
having come here for Kayo's sake, for the marriage's last great gift.
It's too terrible, heat, sweat, flies, death,
blood running in bucketfuls out of the car.
At night I eat the game I watch die slowly.
The doctor writes poems to her,
makes copies for her. He's fallen into her wildness,
her wet summer madness, her tiger eye, tender machine,
all instinct and language stammering her body,
untying the cold, intensive heart,
that mystified, smoky-eyed, trance-heavy heart,
that heart that beats! Blood has to go somewhere.
Each morning on safari she and Kayo wake in an eyeless,
remarkable dark, so he can stalk one perfect impala,
reddish-brown like a summer tan, exquisite horns shaped in a lyre.
The female impala twitches like a question, and she wanders,
hungry, curious, widening each delighted eye.
Territory is an abstraction of grass shoots, of available water,
a mating dance of cocktails and Thorazine.
On the portable typewriter, Anne's tan hands
spread out their fine bones in her amnesia of love,
while zebras move in and out of Kayo's gun sight,
tossing their pretty hair and cantering inked bodies,
their brief, incendiary hammers ringing angry and sublime.

During His Admission Procedure at Abbott Hospital's Mental Health Unit, John Berryman Discourses on The Scarlet Letter's Reverend Dimmesdale

During his admission procedure at Abbott Hospital's mental health unit,
John Berryman discourses on *The Scarlet Letter*'s Reverend Dimmesdale,
on Dimmesdale's crisis and his hidden guilt. Take notes, doctor:
A woman's heart, fastened in her form
like a meager gear hung on wet ribbon,
makes a sound like a quail beneath a blanket of leaves,
so mysterious, so pudgy. It cries and turns,
this lamentation unhooking the male's tangled shape.
Her wants are steel machinery, a gear fish
struggling for the man's sea line, his spine
that stiffens so to hold her, take notes, beware!
She is all language on the inside.

He preachified on the Reverend's pain. He sermonized:
A man weakens, being fatherless,
and torment's aperture widens under its own power,
photo etching, burning me from the inside.
I've got ampersands in my ventricle, idling.
I've got ths and tht in my emptiness, he said,
unhinged in his fusillades of pain. O wild infant,
oh spell unbroken. Wilt thou kiss me now?

The orderly took Berryman's vitals, tried to find
that sodden pulse tip-toeing through the hard hallways of vein,
a temperature insulated in his combustible blood.
Father absence radiates the clumsy, archival heart.
In the hospital ashtray, cigarettes' iron carbide waves
of pleasure and disobedience collide with purity in pure air.
O Doctor the sonnets are killing me, he should have said.

When Anne Sexton Visits Her Therapist, She Tucks Her Red Nightie into Her Purse like Grace Kelly in Rear Window

When Anne Sexton visits her therapist, she tucks her red nightie into her
    purse
like Grace Kelly in *Rear Window*. She'll change in his office
in slow motion, unhooking her Playtex in frames,
the city diffuse, a grid with tiny lives, murmuring.
Kelly enters twenty minutes into the action
through a rose color gel. *Preview of coming attractions*
she says to Jimmy Stewart's Jeff in the film,
pulling pink chiffon from her Mark Cross bag
like she's spinning silk. A girl's got strategies
for fashioning her shameful, spidery hothouse,
her legs' high noon. She's weaving your night out of girl sugars.

Anne Sexton is french-kissing her therapist in a cloud of Arpège,
trancing with her analyst man, city-sweet, her Salem simmering,
the chiffon nightie discarded now. Is that you, poetry?
Are you alright? Everything wrapped around something
like roots or vines, for air, for light.
Translucence made their naked bodies
nearly elegant, lighting the warm lamps, one by one.
In the morning she'd been out in the suburbs,
killing the dandelions before each tiny seed launched
careless on sheer parachutes, a hostile design
that looks so pretty from far away. Bombs away,
Weston, Mass! The kitchen laminate is glossy,
but dirt is dirt, it's nature, damn it,
the rude weeds push up right through your blueprints.
When Anne leaves the office, she'll arrange her hose
so the seams run like arrows up those unbeatable legs,

or she won't bother wearing them at all.
I'll be seeing you in all the old familiar places.
I'll be looking at the moon. American poetry blots its lips,
takes a sedative, has one for the road.

Anne Sexton Watches the Bird Feeder

for the agitation of birds. It is almost too cool
for them to alight. Their sudden fluttering
can surprise, like anything, if you let it terrify.
Outside the house she waits, watching
under the valued sky, staring a craving eye.

A lawn sprinkler satisfies the grass edge.
The ledge of it is an ending. The water exceeds
where it should, not by desire; it overlaps by design.
It floods, it swims, it sprays in delight;
find the metaphor there. Her trained hair

shakes down. She was thinking of turning back
to the old ways, when time galloped its pleasure,
and she held on by being. Now she waits,
turning that marvelous face, that white bone chapter.
How beautiful you'd find it, those eyes opening,

that gin clarity. She is hungry and carved
as a carousel horse is carved,
painted and crucified by its own delightful ribbons.
Here she is, pulling one cigarette from the pack.
There is her wet eye, like a crow's, starved.

She had been in love again but love
sets nothing on fire for long enough.
Now the birds slow and tackle the post,
hungry. They visit as if to chapel, take one seed
and fly away. It's their nearness

that catches her. She would like to touch
down to skin, under feather, the trailing edge

of that pale flashing. They could partake
of one another. She would like to touch
the bird's intimate flight muscles,

the bumps where the feather barbed,
pins itself to skin. How would it be
to toy with that repetitive heart?
Around noon, when she filled it with seed,
the feeder echoed, cried. *What communion*

hath light with darkness? said the air, unkind.
The small beautiful might visit such an altar.
The birds are decisive. They tithe by flying.
She watches them show off and dive,
and take for need. And then she goes inside.

After Sylvia Plath Puts on Her Blue and Silver Cocktail Dress
9 FEBRUARY 1963

After Sylvia Plath puts on her blue and silver cocktail dress
she'll go out for the night, but she won't say where,
passing through the Becker's front door as the afternoon
changes its brilliant mind again. From the sitting room,
the women had watched the sun's temporary net of gold
warm the garden and then abandon it the next minute
in that shameful, isochronal way the world has
of disappointing you. This is how it's been:
her moods warm in the pills until dawn,
sleep broken by that cold cyclical rage, and later,
Beethoven on the phonograph,
the needle mortifying the vinyl repeatedly,
the vinyl fluttering back,
and air, that old what-have-you,
undulating, acute and grave.
The needle reworks the furrow in cycles,
wearing at the hollow like it's obsessed.
Or is it that the album keeps trembling back?
And why wouldn't you want to pulse that track again,
the two of you, a tearing of the skin of gods?
At some point, the brain would relinquish the body,
bored by its disobedience, don't you think, American poetry?
But it's such a pretty dress on her!
Cooled by the night's monochrome, she's gardenia,
with its caustic hospital eye, that intractable flower
that suffers from the human touch, the once-glossy leaves
dropping decisively, giving up. And the unhoused green
she varies into, each forward, astonished step.

Before Theodore Roethke Prepares the Mint Juleps
4 AUGUST 1963

Before Theodore Roethke prepares the mint juleps
he studies the mint, each aromatic leaf.
The plants spread silky runners and invent their confidence
upward to the pure breakthrough, to the wide perennial world,
and their cuttings will run again elsewhere, cold tubers
developing with the parent plant, suffering off into new shoots.
Then Roethke considers the lilies of the field,
wrestling underground, how the creeping root-stock forces,
without ease, its sheath and blades upward,
and knotting bits of fiber circle its head; they droop with weight;
the stem arches, and the knots open to white, stunning bells.
The Bible scribes say *they toil not, they spin not.*
Don't kid yourself, chum, in plants as in poems.
There was worry enough and that's why the flowering.
Consider the mint, for its seed irritated to a flourishing cluster,
for its fine slender body, for its tiny, remarkable crown.
And don't be confused by ideals or the solace of temporary beauty,
of a rosebud's delicate pink, tight with what-have-you,
whose source is the obstinate anchor root.
It's not celebration but stubbornness that saves you,
that weighs and hoists your ballast,
delivers your tangle and your untangle, all resolving to flesh,
all willing to repent. At a certain point, American poetry,
the offshoot separates itself from the stem.
Or is it the other way around? He carries the drinks outside
to the pool, soothed by the day, by the rose's
persistent, returning bloom. Bred for beauty,
each painful arch spread out and frilling like a beast.

When Delmore Schwartz Steps Across the Elevator Transom
11 JULY 1966

When Delmore Schwartz steps across the elevator transom
something ticks and realigns, the tradition of the elevator car
responding to him at four in the morning,
glowing all the old metals to an imaginary bronze.
An elevator takes no notice of suffering.
He had wandered in the wilderness among the betrayers,
the chosen one, assembling his offering of articles,
arguments, midrashim, litigation:
everything piled, everything tinder.
In his Bible stories he was the son to be sacrificed,
scrambling up the mountaintop, awash in conflicting loves,
stiff with his father's binds, reclined on the altar,
an abundance of idleness elsewhere.
He was also the ram: wrong place, wrong time.
In the beginning, conceived in a dream and then hidden,
as a red infant tangled in reeds, he wept in bursts:
one part exuberance, one part fuel, a tiny red apostle.
And what does Isaac say to Abraham
on the way back down the mountain, after the fire
and the scent of Egyptian thorn? American poetry,
what is a good son? Delmore's heart
works its compromises: gather and surrender,
empty and fill, pulse and relent, tithing to invisibles.

While John Berryman Crosses the Washington Avenue Bridge
6 JANUARY 1972

While John Berryman crosses the Washington Avenue Bridge,
he's reading, midway though Hastings' *Encyclopedia of Religion and Ethics*,
Volume 23, Suffering to Transmigration. He's straddling everything:
mid-bridge, below the provisional clouds
that are themselves suspended above the planetary body;
above the land and water, onto which falls
a snow that surrounds him, also in mid-whiteness.
And beneath the appalling snow
are hibernating animals and dormant plants
also passing from one state to another.
To all the materials of triumphant, damaged craftsmanship,
Berryman genuflects to his triumphant, damaged craftsman.
It had been when he was coming down Pike's Peak weeks earlier
that he felt lucky, happier than ever, absorbed among the mysteries,
the perfect green anointing him, provision for the journey.
This should be the last word, before Selah. Bless everybody.
Obligato, Your Majesty. His four-pack-a-day heart
flows its meager reds from one channel to the other,
as the Mississippi wanders just so toward that gulf,
in the middle of everything, yielding itself to the greater waters,
toward that smothering open sea.
The tributary flows toward the parent always,
shaped by what it encounters, modified, patient,
crooked, meandering, lonely, seeking to be absorbed,
pure at heart. How do I love thee, American poetry?
Christ too was in medio, while beauty looked elsewhere,
bored by the fall of every unremarkable, trifling sparrow.
Who accounts for the pain of the obedient son?
Pain like that sees you and raises repeatedly,

until you are stripped clean of having to endure,
until you are bare in thy guilt, unadorned,
sparkling and simplified, received.

While Anne Sexton Is Driving away
4 OCTOBER 1974

While Anne Sexton is driving away,
she rolls down the window to call out to her friend Maxine
something that gets lost in the world's smooth facade
and the car's agitation. But it sounds like her:
shivery as her charm bracelet,
with a catch in her voice, and rough like chiffon,
that scratchy fabric slippery and restless
around her high-strung legs and above,
veiling her voyager hungers.
Anne is driving away, calling out something to Maxine.
It might have been that she'd left her Salems
behind her therapist's vase of daises,
done with the menthol kiss, done
with the ads that promised springtime's gift,
the couples in nature who were not exiled,
who could smoke and harvest bliss
and didn't struggle with loneliness.
(To be happy in the harness of an unseen God.
His muscular love. His thighs and hips.)
Anne calls out the car window
to Maxine, words thinning in all that air.
It might have been how the chickadees
she loved to watch outside her kitchen window
would take from her feeder black oil seeds
and hammer the husk for the softer heart,
each brittle coat breaking for need.
Every bird flies out to show its strength,
angling passions in the air's heat,
casting a pattern in turbulent sweeps to protect
whatever it cherishes in whatever nest it loves:
the little births, the turning points, inconstancy, you name it.

It tries to love in vicissitude. It sings, equally feverish,
to a lover, to a thief, and that song grows spare.
How can history capture the variables, when need
keeps recycling and dredging the hungers,
blurring the camera's passive stare?
Anne Sexton is driving away,
pulling the wheel in a confident arc,
unyielding, on her way, stunning, willed,
shaping the leveling dark with her bright want still wild.

When Robert Lowell Flies Over the Ocean
12 SEPTEMBER 1977

When Robert Lowell flies over the ocean to America,
he's thinking of metaphor, soundings on the brain
like dolphins within the continental shelf,
fluid textures riding restless waves.
He's thinking of his wives and countless loves
in horizontal wildness, turning their sex lathes.
He's thinking of his past, of memory and history,
and of painting and verisimilitude:
Vermeer's play of light, alive across a map;
how birds flew down to peck at Zeuxis' painted grapes.
Could poetry do as much, with its narrative drawling,
its long-distance relationship between subject and word,
and history's verbatim of the eye?

In the cab from the airport, he carries on his lap
Lucien Freud's *Girl in Bed*. Her elongated blue eyes
abide above her bones, votive in the new world.
At Castine Lowell had been at the edge of invention,
anchored in austere blues
—the water's depth, the sky's mid-distance stare—
between heaven and allegory, everything churning in his wake,
the Atlantic collapsing and revising, scraping the shore
like his own blood recycling in his heart.
The car's pulling over on 67th, all that history
coming to rest now for good.
In the painting the woman's skin seems radiant,
in confounding grace, while the real sun
glazes the cab with its transient light.

Elizabeth Bishop Looks Across to Dartmouth Hospital
11 MAY 1979

Elizabeth Bishop looks across to Dartmouth Hospital,
where her Mother had stayed for eighteen years,
then turns her mind inward towards the tall
flowers on this island: False Foxglove,
its capsuled fruit, and Blue Flag's bending spathes,
and Ladies' Tresses—they're only found here,
the white mouths flare politely above ground.
The world is a mist, and then the world
is bright and clear. The clouds are braille
beneath which birds obsessively believe
they are flying, finally, toward sweet houses.
Hunger's grammar steers them: obsessive close-up.
But from here, each pigment blurs, panics dissolve,
and need seems pretty, weaving this way, that way.

Notes

Page 3: 1911. Brett Miller, *Elizabeth Bishop: Life and the Memory of It*, 3.

Page 4: 1912/13. Allan Seager, *The Glass House: The Life of Theodore Roethke*, 19–20, 22–23.

Page 5: 1914. Miller, 5.

Page 6: 1916. Miller, 10–11.

Page 7: 1921–24. James Atlas, *Delmore Schwartz: the Life of an American Poet*, 13–14; Delmore Schwartz, *Genesis*, xx; William H. Pritchard, *Randall Jarrell: A Literary Life*, 16. Note: date possibly 1924 in Stephen Burt, *Randall Jarrell and His Age*, 3.

Page 9: January 4, 1932. Paul Alexander, *Rough Magic: A Biography of Sylvia Plath*, 19.

Page 11: April 25, 1934. Miller, 59.

Page 12: November 11, 1935, Seager, 90–92.

Page 13: 1936. Seager, 101.

Page 14: 1939. Atlas, 151.

Page 15: December 1939. Atlas, 157.

Page 17: 1940–42. Ian Hamilton, *Robert Lowell: A Biography*, 62–64, 80.

Page 18: 1943. Bishop: Miller, 171; Berryman and encyclopedia: John Haffenden, *The Life of John Berryman*,144; Berryman and Palisades: Eileen Simpson, *Poets in their Youth: A Memoir*, 52; John Hershel on relation of polished surfaces, F. Twyman, *Prism and Lensmaking*, 50.

Page 20: August 15, 1946, Robert Lowell, *The Letters of Robert Lowell*, 52; Jean Stafford, "Influx of Poets," *The Collected Stories of Jean Stafford,* 465.

Page 21: November 21, 1951. Miller, 240.

Page 22: 1952. Atlas, 308; see also Saul Bellow, *Humboldt's Gift.*

Page 24: 1952. Princeton estrangement: Atlas, 308; pigeon, Bellow, 123; fall of 1952, Atlas, 308.

Page 25: June/July 1954. Hamilton, 218; the lines "Gothic bride, all arches, groins and stone lace-work, narrow" are from Robert Lowell's "Near the Unbalanced Aquarium," *Robert Lowell: Collected Prose*, 347.

Page 26: 1954. Mariani, 11, 283, 292.

Page 28: 1954. Mariani, 282–83.

Page 29: 1954. Lowell: Cincinnati and May, Dale Brown, "When Poets Were Hip," 96; Gaiety and taxi, Hamilton, 209; Plath deflowered in Cambridge, Plath, *The Unabridged Journals of Sylvia Plath*, 438; see also *The Bell Jar.*

Page 30: New Year's Eve 1955–56. Plath, *Unabridged Journals* 547–549.

Page 32: March 1956. Plath, *Unabridged Journals*, 561. "I am riding the horses one by one and breaking them in": 561; "underpleats": 516.

Page 33: 1952–56. Schwartz: May 31, 1952 and New York Giants, Delmore Schwartz, *Portrait of Delmore: Journals and Notes of Delmore Schwartz, 1939–1959*, 403; in Baptistown, Simpson, 216, Bellow, 23; Willie Jones, Al Dark, and Shibe Park, baseballreference.com. Plath: August 17, 1956, Plath, *Unabridged Journals*, 258, Diana Middlebrook, *Her Husband*, 88.

Page 35: 1957. Atlas, 340.

Page 36: 1957. Diana Middlebrook, *Anne Sexton: A Biography*, 53, 129; cookie flour: James Wright's letter to Sexton.

Page 37: 1955/57. William Barrett, "Delmore: A 30's Friendship and Beyond," 51.

Page 38: 1956. Sexton: Linda Sexton, *Searching for Mercy Street*, 70; Middlebrook, *Anne Sexton*, 162. Lowell: January 1956, Paul Mariani, *Lost Puritan: A Life of Robert Lowell*, 244.

Page 40: 1957–58. Middlebrook, *Anne Sexton*, 47.

Page 41: August 1957. Mariani, *Dream Song*, 319.

Page 42: 1959. Middlebrook, *Anne Sexton*, 119, 122.

Page 44: 1961. Berryman: summer of 1961, Madeline DeFrees, "Resolution and Independence: John Berryman's Ghost and the Meaning of Life." Plath: Chalcot Square flat, Yehuda Koren and Eliat Negev, *Lover of Unreason: Assia Wevill, Sylvia Plath's Rival and Ted Hughes' Doomed Love*, 81.

Page 46: 1962. Plath: summer 1962, Middlebrook, 173–74. Schwartz: Autumn 1962, Atlas, 366.

Page 47: June 1962. Hamilton, 303.

Page 48: May 1962. Berryman: Mariani, *Dream Song*, Don Quixote, 76: 2 linear feet of manuscript, 377.

Page 50: 1962/1963. Plath kicks out Hughes, October 11, 1962, Alexander, 298; Bishop watches police chase thief, April 1963, Miller, 345.

Page 51: October 1962. Anne Stevenson, *Bitter Fame: A Life of Sylvia Plath*, 275.

Page 52: August 1963. Elizabeth Bishop and Robert Lowell, *Words in Air: the Complete Correspondence between Elizabeth Bishop and Robert Lowell*, 486.

Page 53: February 9, 1964. Linda Gray Sexton, *Anne Sexton: A Self-Portrait in Letters*, 231–32.

Page 54: January/February 1965. Hamilton, 316–18.

Page 55: August 1966. Middlebrook, *Anne Sexton: A Biography*, 262–63.

Page 56: November 1967. Mariani, *Dream Song*, 433–34.

Page 57: 1966–69. Middlebrook, *Anne Sexton: A Biography*, 313.

Page 61: 1963. Jillian Becker, *Giving Up: The Last Days of Sylvia Plath*, Plath's blue and silver dress, 3; Saturday, 14; sun's gold, 36; Beethoven, 26.

Page 62: 1963. Seager, 285.

Page 63: 1966. Atlas, 376.

Page 64: 1972. Berryman observed crossing the Washington Avenue Bridge reading Hastings the day before he died, Mariani, *Dream Song*, 500; Pikes Peak and Selah, John Berryman, *Recovery*, 142.

Page 66: 1974. Middlebrook, *Anne Sexton: A Biography*, chickadees, 395, Maxine Kumin and car, 396.

Page 68: 1977. 67th Street, Mariani, *Lost Puritan*, 460; painting, Hamilton, 473; the painting was *Girl in Bed*, Kathryn Hughes, "Lucian Freud's Fragile Beauty: the Life of Lady Caroline Blackwood," *The Telegraph*, February 8, 2012.

Page 69: 1979, Bishop looking at Dartmouth Hospital as she receives an honorary degree from Dalhousie University several months before her death, Miller, 547; May 11, "Elizabeth Bishop at Dalhousie University Convocation," *Chronicle-Herald*, 11; the lines "The world is a mist and then the world is / minute and vast and clear," are from Elizabeth Bishop's "The Sandpiper," *Elizabeth Bishop: the Complete Poems 1927–1979*, 131.

Bibliography

Alexander, Paul. *Rough Magic: A Biography of Sylvia Plath*. New York: Viking, 1991.

Atlas, James. *Delmore Schwartz: the Life of an American Poet*. New York: Farrar, Straus and Giroux, 1977.

Barrett, William. "Delmore: A 30's Friendship and Beyond," *Commentary* 1 Sept. 1974: 41–54.

Becker, Jillian. *Giving Up: The Last Days of Sylvia Plath*. New York: St. Martins, 2003.

Bellow, Saul. *Humboldt's Gift*. New York: Viking, 1975.

Berryman, John. *Recovery*. New York: Farrar, Straus and Giroux, 1973.

Bishop, Elizabeth. "The Sandpiper." *Elizabeth Bishop: the Complete Poems 1927–1979*. New York: Farrar, Straus and Giroux, 1983. 131.

—. and Robert Lowell. *Words in Air: the Complete Correspondence between Elizabeth Bishop and Robert Lowell*. Ed. Thomas Travisano with Saskia Hamilton. New York: Farrar, Straus and Giroux, 2010.

Brown, Dale. "When Poets Were Hip." *Cincinnati Magazine* 36.9 (2003): 96.

Burt, Stephen. *Randall Jarrell and His Age*. New York: Columbia University Press, 2003.

DeFrees, Madeline. "Resolution and Independence: John Berryman's Ghost and the Meaning of Life." *The Gettysburg Review* 9.7 (1996): 9–29.

"Elizabeth Bishop at Dalhousie University Convocation." *Chronicle-Herald* 12 May 1979: 11.

Haffenden, John. *The Life of John Berryman*. Boston: Routledge & Kegan Paul, 1982.

Hamilton, Ian. *Robert Lowell: A Biography*. New York: Random House, 1982.

Hughes, Kathryn. "Lucian Freud's Fragile Beauty: the Life of Lady Caroline Blackwood." *The Telegraph* 8 February 2012. Web.

Koren, Yehuda, and Eliat Negev. *Lover of Unreason: Assia Wevill, Sylvia Plath's Rival and Ted Hughes' Doomed Love*. Cambridge: Da Capo, 2008.

Lowell, Robert. *Collected Prose*. Ed. Robert Giroux. New York: Farrar, Straus, Giroux, 1987.

—. *The Letters of Robert Lowell*. Ed. Saskia Hamilton. New York: Farrar, Straus and Giroux, 2005.

Mariani, Paul. L. *Dream Song: The Life of John Berryman*. New York: William Morrow, 1990.

—. *Lost Puritan: A Life of Robert Lowell*. New York: W. W. Norton, 1954.

Middlebrook, Diana. *Anne Sexton: A Biography*. New York: Vintage, 1992.

—. *Her Husband: Ted Hughes and Sylvia Plath—A Marriage*. New York: Penguin, 2003.

Miller, Brett. *Elizabeth Bishop: Life and the Memory of It*. Berkeley: University of California Press, 1993.

Plath, Sylvia. *The Bell Jar*. New York: HarperCollins, 2006.

—. *The Unabridged Journals of Sylvia Plath 1950–1962*. Ed. Karen V. Kukil. New York: Anchor, 2000.

Pritchard, William H. *Randall Jarrell: A Literary Life*. New York: Farrar, Straus and Giroux, 1990.

Schwartz, Delmore. *Genesis*. New York: J. Laughlin, 1943.

—. *Portrait of Delmore: Journals and Notes of Delmore Schwartz 1939–1959*. Ed. Elizabeth Pollet. New York: Farrar, Straus and Giroux, 1986.

Seager, Allan. *The Glass House: The Life of Theodore Roethke*. New York: McGraw-Hill, 1968.

Sexton, Anne. *Anne Sexton: A Self-Portrait in Letters*. Eds. Lois Ames and Linda Grey Sexton. New York: Mariner, 2004.

Sexton, Linda. *Searching for Mercy Street*. New York: Little Brown, 1994.

Simpson, Eileen. *Poets in their Youth: A Memoir*. New York: Random House, 1982.

Stafford, Jean. *The Collected Stories of Jean Stafford*. New York: Farrar, Straus and Giroux, 1969.

Stevenson, Anne. *Bitter Fame: A Life of Sylvia Plath*. Boston: Houghton Mifflin, 1989.

F. Twyman. *Prism and Lensmaking*. London: Hilger & Watts, 1952

Wright, James. Letter to Anne Sexton, 12 August, 1960. University of Texas, Harry Ransom Center.

Acknowledgments

I'm grateful to the editors of the following journals and magazines where these poems first appeared: *Berkeley Poetry Review, Carbon Copy, The Chronicle of Higher Education, Fifth Wednesday, The Gettysburg Review, Great River Review, Green Mountains Review, Hotel Amerika, Indiana Review, The Laurel Review, The Missouri Review, Narrative, POOL, The Rumpus,* and *Southern Indiana Review.*

Several of these poems have been reprinted, in *Drunken Boat, The Fickle Grey Beast, Heart of the Order: Baseball Poems, The Hide-and-Seek Muse: A Year of Chronicle Columns & Commentaries on Contemporary American Poetry, The Missouri Review*'s *TextBox: Online Anthology and Resource for Creative Writing, The Rumpus Original Poetry Anthology,* and at the Illinois Poet Laureate site.

Gratitude to the staff at the Harry Ransom Center at the University of Texas at Austin, and to Northern Illinois University for a Summer Grant in Research and Artistry and a Presidential Research Professorship which aided in the completion of the book.

Thanks to my editor, Gabe Fried, for the care and attention he's given these poems. Thanks to Joe, Molly, and Dan, who understand.